MACHINES AT WORK

Cars and Bikes

IAN GRAHAM

QEB Publishing, Inc.

Copyright © QEB Publishing Inc. 2007

First published in the United States in 2007 by
QEB Publishing Inc.
23062 La Cadena Drive
Laguna Hills, CA 92653
www.qeb-publishing.com

Library of Congress Control Number: 2006933234

ISBN 978-1-59566-317-7

Written by Ian Graham
Produced by Calcium
Editor Sarah Medina
Fold-out illustration by Ian Naylor
Picture Researcher Maria Joannou

Publisher Steve Evans
Creative Director Zeta Davies
Senior Editor Hannah Ray

Printed and bound in China

Picture credits

Key: T = top, B = bottom, C = center, L = left, R = right, FC = front cover

Alamy Images/Jack Cox/Travel Pics Pro 29, /Motoring Picture Library 14; **Aston Martin** 7T; **Audi** 8; **Aurora Vehicle Association Inc** 27B; **Auto Express** 6–7; **Chevrolet**/General Motors 9; **Conceptcarz.com**/Dan Vaughan 33; **Corbis** 26–27, /Jo Lillini 24–25, /David Madison 21, /Nigel Marple 24, /Charles O'Rear 4, /Schlegelmilch 16, /Shannon Stapleton 15, /George Tiedemann 17T, 20T, /Tim de Waele 13T, /Cathrine Wessel 13B; **DaimlerChrysler** 14–15; **Department of Defence Visual Information Center** 11; **Duncan McQueen** photo of bike designed by Sam Jilbert BA (Hons) Transportation design, Northumbria University Newcastle 32; **Getty Images** 10–11, /AFP 25, /AFP/Jean-Francois Monier 8-9, /Jack Atley 28–29, /John Chapple 30–31, 31, /Jon Ferrey 22, /Jeff Gross 20B, /Gavin Lawrence 16–21, /Sterling Marlin 17B, /Bill Pugliano 32–33, /Reportage/Jamie McDonald 12–13; **Istockphoto**/David Olah 28, /Pamela Hodson 5; **Jeep**/DaimlerChrysler 10; **NHRA** 22–23, 23; **Photos.com** 4–5; **Porsche** 7B, **Rex Features**/Erik C. Pendzich 30; **Tu Delft University of Technology** 27T

Words in **bold** can be found in the Glossary on page 34.

CONTENTS

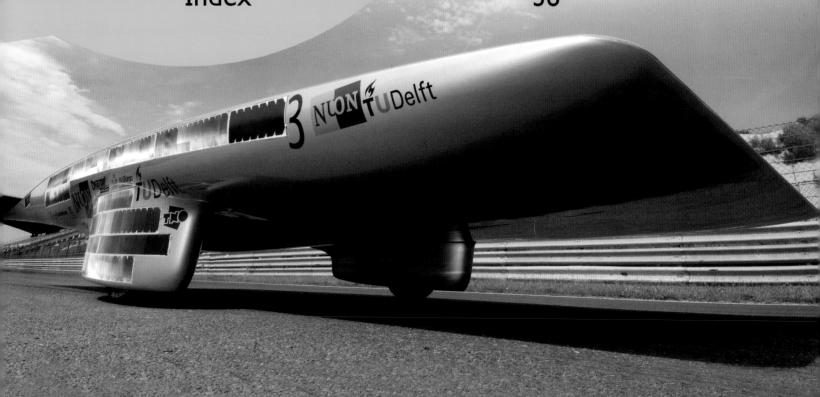

CARS AND BIKES

More than 500 million cars drive along the world's roads today, and the number is growing all the time. Cars come in all shapes and sizes, from family cars and people carriers to **sports cars**, off-road cars, and **supercars**. There are many millions of motorbikes and cycles, too. Cars and motorbikes give people freedom to travel, but there are so many vehicles now that traffic jams often cause delays at busy times.

Building cars

Most cars are made from steel parts **welded** together. In a modern car factory, robots do this work. They also move parts into position to be fitted to cars. People still do all the trickier work needed to finish off each vehicle, for example, putting in the seats.

▼ Robots build cars on a factory production line.

robot

ENGINE POWER

Most cars and motorbikes are driven by engines that burn a fuel such as gasoline. The gasoline is sprayed into a tube-shaped cylinder. A spark sets the fuel on fire. The air heats up and expands, which pushes a tight-fitting piston down the cylinder. Pistons moving like this in four or more cylinders provide the force to drive the car or motorbike's wheels.

The **power** to drive a car comes ➤ from its engine. The driver makes the engine go faster by pressing a pedal.

FACT!
By the year 2050, there could be nearly a **billion** cars on the world's roads.

▲ Road transport is essential for our modern way of life.

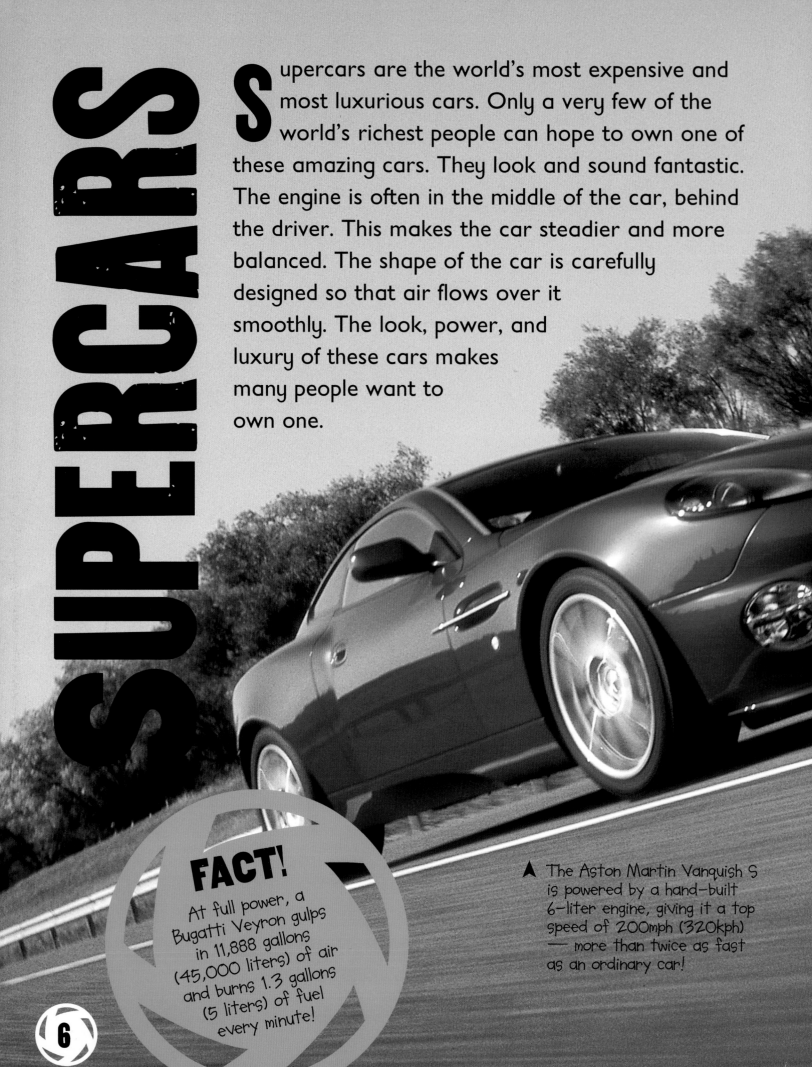

SUPERCARS

Supercars are the world's most expensive and most luxurious cars. Only a very few of the world's richest people can hope to own one of these amazing cars. They look and sound fantastic. The engine is often in the middle of the car, behind the driver. This makes the car steadier and more balanced. The shape of the car is carefully designed so that air flows over it smoothly. The look, power, and luxury of these cars makes many people want to own one.

FACT!

At full power, a Bugatti Veyron gulps in 11,888 gallons (45,000 liters) of air and burns 1.3 gallons (5 liters) of fuel every minute!

▲ The Aston Martin Vanquish S is powered by a hand-built 6-liter engine, giving it a top speed of 200mph (320kph) — more than twice as fast as an ordinary car!

rear wing

Bugatti Veyron

Everything about the Bugatti Veyron is mind-boggling. It has a huge engine that is actually two normal car engines side-by-side. They give the Veyron a top speed of 250mph (400kph). At high speed, a wing rises up at the back of the car to hold it steady on the road.

▲ The Bugatti Veyron's beautiful body is made from a material called **carbon fiber**.

PORSCHE'S SUPERCAR

The Porsche Carrera GT goes from zero to 62mph (100kph) in less than four seconds. Most cars take two or three times longer than this. The power for this great performance is supplied by a 605-horsepower **engine** behind the driver, which is three or four times more powerful than a family car.

▲ Only a few hundred Porsche Carrera GT supercars are built every year.

SPORTS CARS

Some people enjoy driving so much that they want a car that is lots of fun to drive. Sports cars are small and fast. They do not have much space for carrying luggage and they usually have just two seats. This makes them shorter than other cars. They are lighter and more **maneuverable**, so they are great fun to drive. Some sports cars have a top that folds down for open-top driving in good weather.

SPORTS RACERS

There are motor races especially for sports cars. Some of the cars that take part are more powerful racing versions of ordinary sports cars. Others are specially designed racing sports cars, such as the Audi R8, which can reach 200mph (320kph) or more.

▲ The open-top Audi R8 is one of the most successful racing sports cars.

Corvette

The first Chevrolet Corvette sports car was built more than 50 years ago, in 1953. It was an instant success. It has been updated, or redesigned, regularly since then. The latest Corvette has a 6-liter, 400-horsepower engine. This is one of the biggest engines in any sports car.

The most powerful sports cars, ▶ such as the Chevrolet Corvette, are sometimes called muscle cars.

▲ The world-famous sports car race held at Le Mans in France goes on for 24 hours — all day and all night!

FACT!
The Mazda MX-5 is the best-selling sports car ever.

OFF-ROAD

Most cars are designed for normal roads. They drive well on dry and wet roads, and they can also cope with firm earth and grass. However, they get stuck easily in soft or muddy ground, which makes their wheels spin and sink. Off-road cars are designed specially for these conditions. There is more space between the ground and the bottom of the car, so they can bump over uneven, rocky ground without getting damaged underneath. They also have special tires to give them more grip.

Power plus

A normal car engine usually drives just the two front wheels or the two back wheels of the car. This two-wheel drive is good for roads, but it does not grip soft ground well. Off-road cars are also called 4x4s (four by fours) or **four-wheel drives**, because the engine drives all four wheels to give extra grip.

4x4 off-road cars have twice ➤ as much grip as other cars.

MULTI-WHEELERS

One way to get better grip on wet or loose ground is to reduce the car's weight and to add more wheels. Some extreme off-roaders have six, or even eight, wheels. They are not the fastest or best-looking vehicles, but they leave other cars far behind in the worst ground conditions.

▲ A car with lots of wheels can grip soft ground better.

▲ Off-road cars make short work of wet or muddy ground.

FACT!
The World War II US Jeep became one of the most famous 4x4 vehicles ever.

PEDAL POWER

Bicycles have existed for about 200 years. Today, cars and motorbikes are faster, but pedal-powered bikes are more popular than ever. They are simple machines that work well and they can be repaired easily. There is no engine, so they do not need to fill up with fuel to work—they are human-powered vehicles (HPVs). The pedals and **gears** on a bike make them easier to ride. Changing gear can make it easier to go faster or cycle uphill. Some bikes have as many as 30 gears.

FACT!
The first mountain bikes were made in the 1970s in the US.

CARBON RACERS

The bikes ridden by racing cyclists in the Olympic Games look different from other bikes. The frame is made from lightweight carbon fiber instead of steel. The wheels have broad blades **instead of wire** spokes, or they may be even more streamlined **solid discs**. These differences make the bikes much faster.

solid disc wheel

▲ Olympic racing bikes are lighter and more streamlined than other bikes.

Mountain bikes

Mountain bikes are designed for riding on rough tracks. They are also called all-terrain bikes. They have a stronger frame and wheels than other bikes, and can bump along rocky ground without bending or breaking. Their fat, knobbly tires give better grip on loose ground.

◄ BMX bikes are small and strong for racing on hilly dirt tracks or for freestyle stunt riding.

▲ Mountain bikes have to be strongly built for rough riding.

RESCUE

Police and medical services use cars and bikes for emergency rescue work. A car can carry people and equipment, but a motorbike is faster. An experienced **paramedic** on a fast motorbike can give life-saving help before an ambulance arrives. A police motorcyclist can speed to a trouble spot, even on roads blocked by traffic jams. Bicycles are useful for this work, too. Police officers and paramedics can cover the ground faster on bicycles than they can on foot.

The US car company Dodge makes ➤ this special police version of its Charger car for police forces.

▲ The Harley-Davidson police motorbike is a favorite with many US police forces.

POLICE BIKES

Police officers on motorcycles are a common sight on the roads. Police motorbikes can squeeze between lines of traffic that hold up police cars. The bikes are specially adapted for police work. They carry extra equipment. As well as flashing lights and a siren, they can be fitted with radar and video equipment to check on other road users.

RACING CARS

Racing cars combine great power, light weight and a streamlined shape. Some racing cars are based on ordinary cars, but they have more powerful engines and stronger bodies for racing. Others, such as **IndyCars**, are specially designed for racing. IndyCars and **Formula 1** cars are **single-seaters**. The car's long, slim body is so low down between the wheels that the driver has to lie on his back to drive the vehicle.

Single-seaters

There is no room for the engine at the front of a single-seat racing car, so it sits behind the driver. The car has wings on its nose and tail to help it to go round corners faster. As the wings slice through the air, they suck the car downward, pressing the tires down harder. This is called **downforce**.

rear wing

nose wing

Wings make IndyCars ➤ faster through turns.

NASCAR

NASCAR racing is the most popular motor sport in the US, with more than 75 million fans. NASCAR stands for the National Association for Stock Car Auto Racing. It started in the 1940s with races between stock, or ordinary, cars. NASCAR cars look a little like ordinary cars, but they are all hand-built especially for racing. They do not have the modern computers or **aerodynamic** bodies that are used in other motor sports, but they have a lot of power. Most NASCAR races are held on oval circuits with sharp turns that make for very exciting races.

Under the hood

NASCAR cars are powered by a 5.87-liter engine. It works exactly like a big ordinary car engine, but it is specially built to produce the maximum power for racing. It is more than twice as powerful as an ordinary car engine of the same size.

◄ NASCAR cars can reach speeds of more than 200 mph (320 kph).

ROOF FLAPS

If a NASCAR race car spins round and slides backward along the track, it could take off like a plane! Flaps on the roof stop this happening. If a car spins, the flaps pop up. This means the car is not the shape of a wing any more, so it does not take off.

Roof-top flaps stop cars from ▲ taking off and flying through the air.

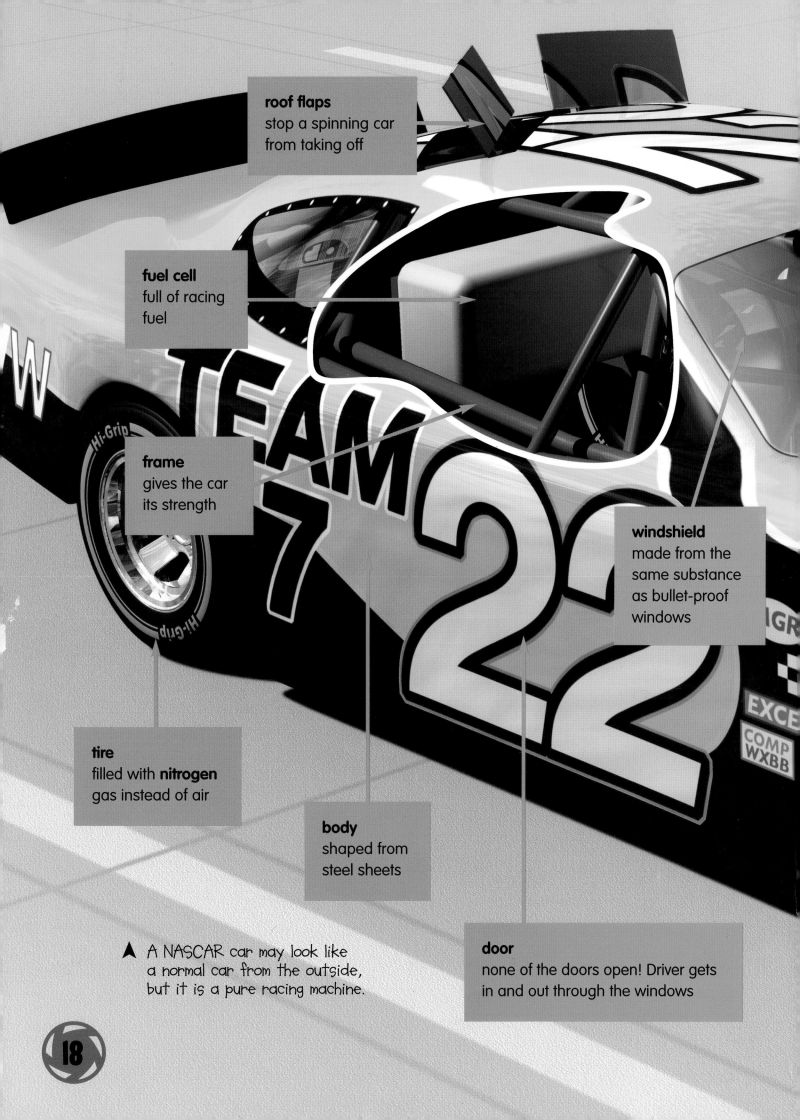

roof flaps
stop a spinning car
from taking off

fuel cell
full of racing
fuel

frame
gives the car
its strength

windshield
made from the
same substance
as bullet-proof
windows

tire
filled with **nitrogen**
gas instead of air

body
shaped from
steel sheets

▲ A NASCAR car may look like
a normal car from the outside,
but it is a pure racing machine.

door
none of the doors open! Driver gets
in and out through the windows

18

Pedal force

Police officers and paramedics on mountain bikes can get round obstructions and through crowds quickly. They can even **patrol** inside big buildings, such as stations and airport terminals, where cars and motorbikes cannot go. They keep in touch with other officers by radio.

▲ Officers on bikes can answer nearby calls quickly.

FACT!

Sea-Tac Airport in Seattle, USA, is patrolled by 20 police officers on mountain bikes.

CHEWY TIRES

A racing car's tires heat up during a race. They can get as hot as boiling water! At that temperature, the rubber is like tar or chewing gum. It sticks to the road better, but it soon starts to break up. That is why cars have to have new wheels fitted during a race.

▲ A racing car's tires may only last 99 miles (160 km) before they have to be changed.

▼ IndyCars are nearly four times as powerful as ordinary cars.

FACT!

At top speed, an IndyCar's front wheels spin more than 40 times every second!

At the wheel

A NASCAR car driver sits in a wrap-around seat that gives extra protection in case a crash happens. The driver is held in the seat by a special harness with five extra-strong seat belts. The side windows are covered with nets to stop parts of the car flying into the driver during a crash.

▲ A driver sits strapped into his seat inside a strong steel cage before a NASCAR race.

Safety first

NASCAR cars are designed to protect the driver if they should crash. The nose and tail of the car are made weaker than the middle. They soak up the impact of a crash by crumpling, while the driver sits inside a super-strong steel cage.

The nose of a NASCAR ▲ racing car is designed to crumple in a crash.

headlights
not real – just for show!

FACT!
A good NASCAR team can re–fuel a car and change all of its wheels in less than 14 seconds!

SUPER-POWER

Dragsters are the fastest and most powerful racing cars. They do not race round circuits like other racing cars. They are designed to do one simple thing—to go as fast as possible in a straight line! The cars race two at a time along a straight track called a **drag strip**. There are different classes of dragsters with their own rules. The long, thin Top Fuel dragsters are fastest and they can go as fast as 336 mph (540 kph).

In the cockpit

The driver's seat of a Top Fuel dragster is a scary place to be. The driver is strapped tightly into a seat inside a steel cage. He wears a fireproof suit and crash helmet.

Smoke and flames ➤ are a normal part of drag races.

FACT!
A Top Fuel dragster race may last as little as five seconds!

◀ A Top Fuel dragster driver sits in a cramped **cockpit** and waits for the signal to go.

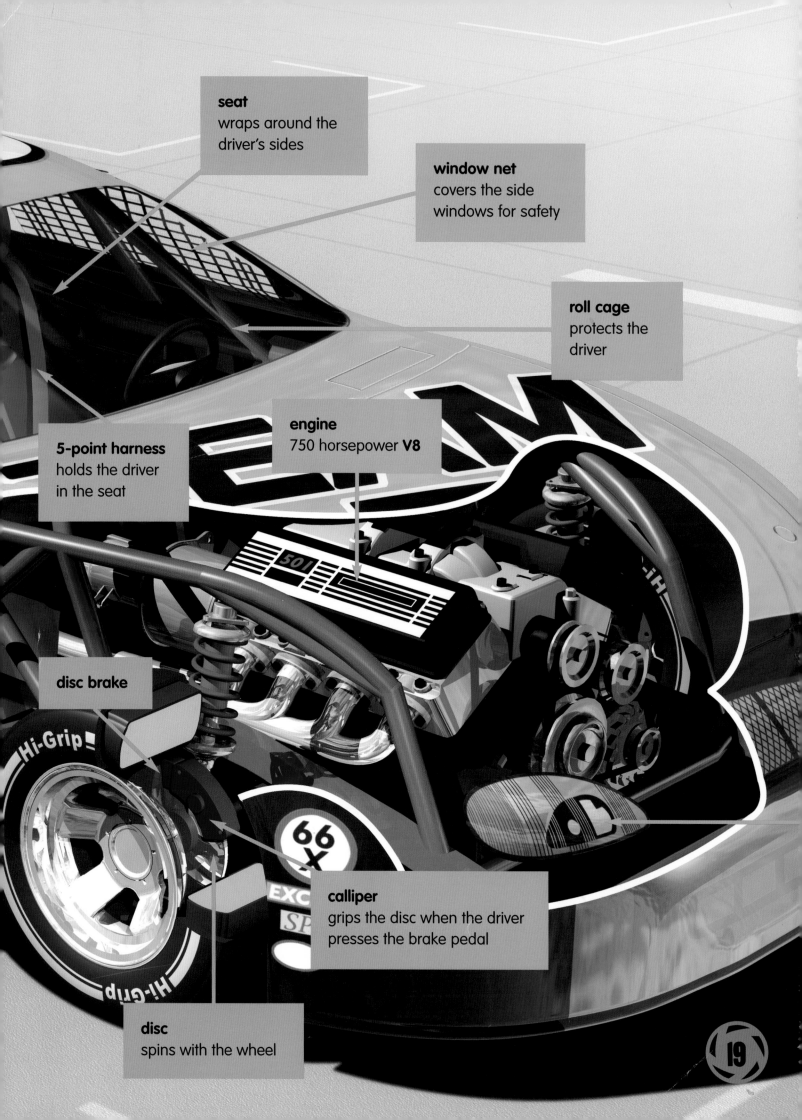

seat
wraps around the
driver's sides

window net
covers the side
windows for safety

roll cage
protects the
driver

engine
750 horsepower **V8**

5-point harness
holds the driver
in the seat

disc brake

calliper
grips the disc when the driver
presses the brake pedal

disc
spins with the wheel

Hi-Grip

Hi-Grip

66
X

EXC

SP

DRAG BIKES

Cars are not the only drag racers. There are drag bikes, too. A drag bike's big back wheel turns with such a great force that it can flip the whole bike over on its back. A long bar trailing behind the bike stops this.

▼ A drag bike rider lies forward on the bike to make a more streamlined shape.

rear wing

engine air intakes

wheelie bar

engine

small front wheels

DIRT DEVILS

I magine driving at 100 mph (160 kph)—faster than in the fast lane of a highway—on slippery roads or in fog. It sounds dangerous, but this is exactly how **rally** cars are driven. Rally drivers set off one by one, and they drive as fast as they can to set the fastest time in each race, or **stage**. They do this on closed roads through forests, countryside, or even mountains! Rally cars look like ordinary cars but they are specially built for rallying.

World rally cars

The cars that take part in the biggest rally, the World Rally Championship, have a 2-liter engine and are three times more powerful than a normal car. Their top speed is about 124 mph (200 kph).

▼ A team of mechanics may have only a few minutes to repair a rally car between stages, no matter what's wrong!

24

INSIDE THE CAR

The car's crew sits inside a strong cage, which stops the roof being flattened if the car turns over. The driver concentrates on driving. The co-driver looks at a map and some notes, and warns the driver about what is coming up ahead, for example, a sharp turn, a rise or a dip in the road.

◀ Rally crews are strapped tightly into their seats by extra-strong seat belts called harnesses.

FACT!

It costs thousands of dollars to produce a World Rally Championship car!

▲ Rally drivers do not slow down over bumps!

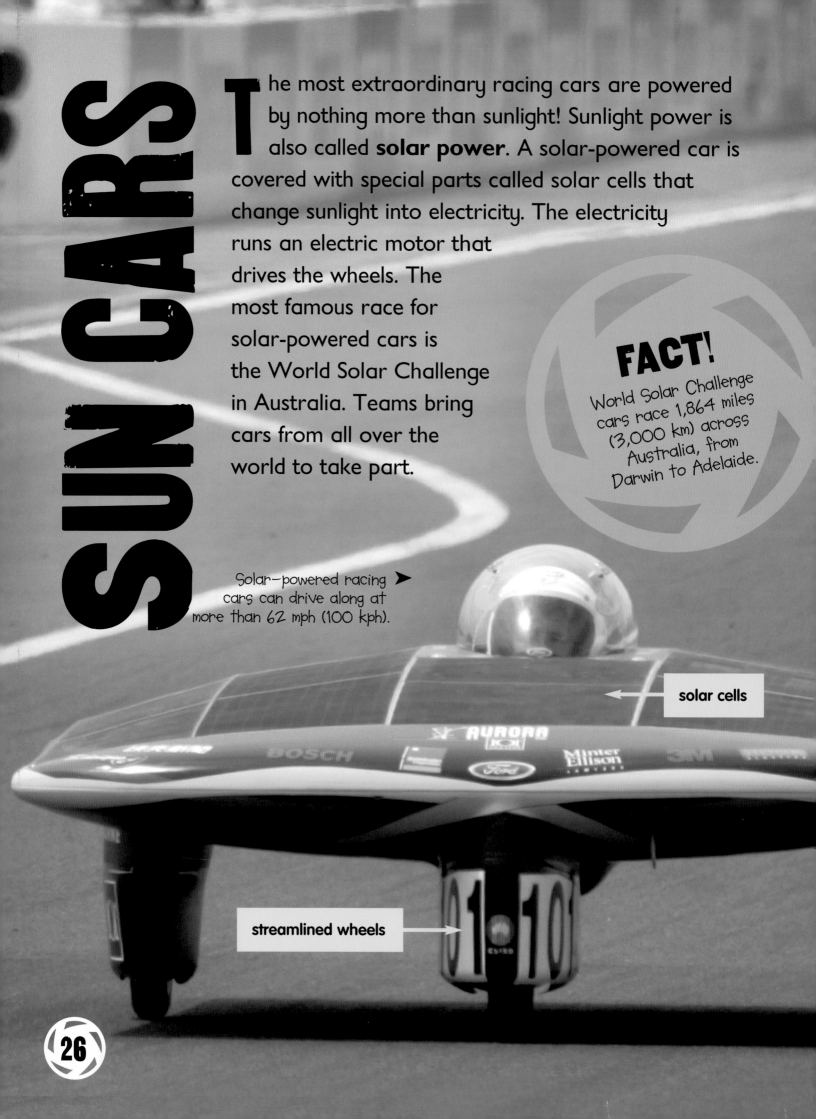

SUN CARS

The most extraordinary racing cars are powered by nothing more than sunlight! Sunlight power is also called **solar power**. A solar-powered car is covered with special parts called solar cells that change sunlight into electricity. The electricity runs an electric motor that drives the wheels. The most famous race for solar-powered cars is the World Solar Challenge in Australia. Teams bring cars from all over the world to take part.

FACT!

World Solar Challenge cars race 1,864 miles (3,000 km) across Australia, from Darwin to Adelaide.

Solar-powered racing cars can drive along at more than 62 mph (100 kph). ➤

solar cells

streamlined wheels

Nuna 3

The 2005 World Solar Challenge race was won by a car from The Netherlands called Nuna 3. The Nuna 3 is a three-wheeled car. The tiny electric motor that drives it is inside the rear wheel. The driver sees the road ahead through a streamlined **plastic bubble** on top of the car.

▲ Every part of Nuna 3 is carefully shaped to reduce **air resistance** that would slow it down.

Aurora made the ➤ longest—ever **solar car** journey by travelling 8,111 miles (13,054 km) around Australia in 24 days.

AURORA

Aurora is an Australian solar racing car. It won the World Solar Challenge race in 1999 and came second four times. The car stands only 37 inches (95cm) high. The driver has to lie down inside its body.

MOTORBIKES

People have been building motorbikes for more than 120 years. Today, there are all sorts of different motorbikes. There are big comfortable cruisers for touring, commuter bikes for short city journeys, specially designed sports bikes, lightweight trail bikes, and super-fast racing bikes. All motorbikes have the same basic layout, because it works well. The engine sits under the seat in the middle of a strong frame called the chassis. The engine usually drives the back wheel by means of a chain.

▲ Motocross riders often fly through the air as they reach the tops of hills.

RACING BIKES

Superbike, MotoGP, and Motocross are all types of motorbike racing. Superbikes are racing versions of ordinary road bikes. MotoGP bikes are designed just for racing. Superbikes and MotoGP races are held on road tracks. Motocross is different. The races are held on hilly dirt tracks. Supercross is a type of Motocross held on specially built indoor dirt tracks.

Touring bikes

Touring bikes are built for long journeys. Their big engines can purr along the roads for hours. They have carriers for luggage, and the upright riding position is comfortable. Some touring bikes even have a built-in sound system to feed music into the rider's helmet!

The Honda Gold Wing is ▲ a popular touring bike.

streamlined **fairing**

FACT!
The Suzuki Hayabusa is the fastest superbike, with a top speed of 195mph (312kph).

▲ A MotoGP rider leans his bike over to make a tight turn.

29

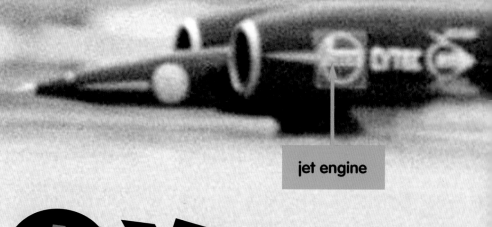

RECORD BREAKERS

The cars and motorbikes that set speed and distance records have two things in common. They have super-powerful engines to boost them to the highest possible speed. They also look like planes or rockets, because these are the best shapes to reduce air resistance. The world's fastest car goes faster than a jet **airliner**, but the team of designers and engineers who built it had to make sure it would not take off like a plane!

jet engine

Easy record

The world's fastest motorbike is called Easyriders. The rider does not sit on top of it like a normal motorbike. Instead, he sits inside its slim body along with two powerful engines. In 1990, Dave Campos set a new world record by taking Easyriders up to 322 mph (518 kph).

The rocket-shaped ➤ motorbikes that set speed records are called **streamliners**.

FASTER THAN SOUND

The record-breaking Thrust SSC car has two engines, but they are not like other car engines. They are jet engines! In 1997, Royal Air Force pilot Andy Green set a new speed record of 762 mph (1,227 kph) in Thrust SSC — faster than the speed of sound.

▲ Thrust SSC is the first **supersonic** car.

▲ The Thrust SSC jet-car is the fastest in the world.

FACT!

Thrust SSC set the first supersonic speed record in the Black Rock Desert in Nevada.

FUTURE

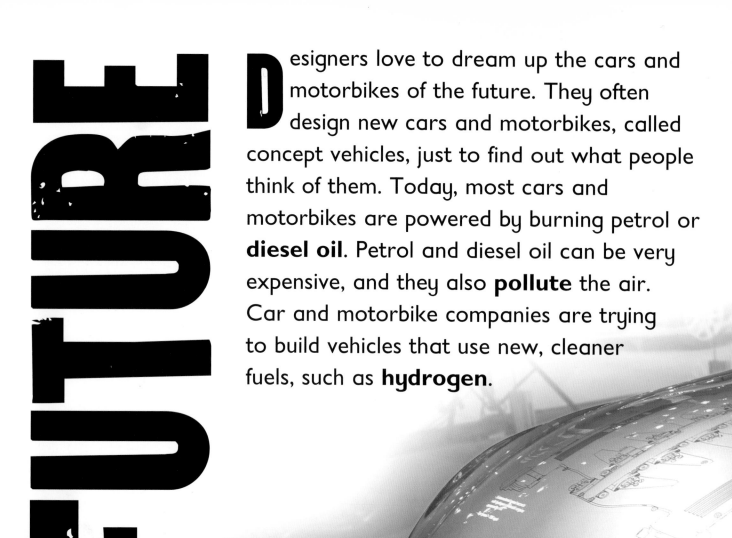

Designers love to dream up the cars and motorbikes of the future. They often design new cars and motorbikes, called concept vehicles, just to find out what people think of them. Today, most cars and motorbikes are powered by burning petrol or **diesel oil**. Petrol and diesel oil can be very expensive, and they also **pollute** the air. Car and motorbike companies are trying to build vehicles that use new, cleaner fuels, such as **hydrogen**.

▲ Future motorbikes could be a completely different shape from today's motorbikes.

FUTURE BIKES

Designers are always trying new shapes and new materials for future vehicles. Motorbikes have always had to be built around a big gasoline engine. By getting rid of the engine and using fuel cells instead, future motorbikes could be made in all sorts of new shapes.

◄ Fuel-cell cars such as this Honda FCX Hydrogen Fuel Concept Car could be on the roads by 2010.

Hydrogen power

Hydrogen is a clean fuel. When it burns in an engine, it produces water. Hydrogen can also be used in a different way, without burning it. It can make electricity in a fuel cell. Electricity from a fuel cell powers an electric motor that drives the car's wheels. Future cars may be powered by fuel cells.

FACT!

Hydrogen-powered fuel cells make electricity in the Space Shuttle.

▲ The BMW HR2 is a futuristic hydrogen-powered racing car that holds nine speed records.

aerodynamic made in the best shape for moving through air as fast as possible

air resistance the slowing effect of air when something tries to move through it. Streamlined shapes cause the least air resistance

airliner an aircraft used by an airline to fly fare-paying passengers

billion one thousand million

blade part of a racing bike's wheels, connecting the center of the wheel to the rim. Unlike spokes, they look thin from the front and wide from the side, like a knife blade

carbon fiber a material that is stronger and lighter than steel

cockpit the part of a racing car where the driver sits

cylinder a tube-shaped part of an engine where the fuel is burned

diesel oil a type of oil burned inside a diesel engine

downforce the downward pressure pressing on a racing car caused by the shape of the car and its wings. Downforce helps the car's tires to grip the ground and go round bends faster without skidding

drag bike a racing bike that takes part in drag races

drag strip a straight racing track about 1,312 ft. (400 m) long where dragsters race two at a time

dragster a drag racing car or bike

expand to become bigger

fairing a streamlined cover fitted around part of a motorbike to reduce air resistance

Formula 1 an international motor-racing championship for single-seat cars built according to the rules called Formula 1

four-wheel drive a car where all four wheels are driven by the engine

fuel a liquid or gas used by an engine or fuel cell to power a vehicle

fuel cell a machine that combines hydrogen and oxygen to make electricity, and also another name for a racing car's fuel tank

gasoline a fuel burned inside most car engines. Also called petrol in the UK

gears toothed wheels. Car and motorbike engines are connected to the road-wheels by a set of gears. Bicycle gears drive a chain, which turns the bike's back wheel. Changing gear changes the speed of the car or bike

horsepower a measurement of power. The power of a car engine is measured in horsepower

hydrogen a gas. Hydrogen is lighter than air and it burns very easily. Future cars will probably use it as a fuel

IndyCar a racing car that takes part in Indy Racing in the US

liter a space equal in size to 61 cubic inches (1000 cc, or cubic centimetres). The size of the cylinders inside an engine, where the fuel burns, is measured in liters, cc, or cubic inches

maneuverable able to be steered easily and quickly

nitrogen a gas. Most of the air around us is made of nitrogen

paramedic a person who provides emergency medical care

patrol to move around a place to watch what is happening there

piston part of an engine, about the size and shape of a drink can, that fits inside a cylinder

pollute to give out smelly or harmful fumes or smoke

power the speed at which energy changes from one form to another form. A more powerful car engine changes fuel energy into movement faster than a less powerful engine

radar equipment used by police officers to check the speed of vehicles

rally a type of race for cars that set off one at a time. The drivers try to set the fastest time. A rally is usually divided into a series of separate timed events called stages

single-seater a car with only one seat, for the driver

solar car a car powered by sunlight

solar power powered by the sun. Solar-powered cars change sunlight into electricity to power a motor

speed of sound the speed at which sound travels through a substance. The speed of sound in air depends on the temperature. On a cool day, the speed of sound in air is about 760 mph (1223 kph)

spoke one of the many thin pieces of metal that connect the center of a wheel to the rim

sports car a small, lightweight, nimble, fast car that's fun to drive

stage one of the timed race events that forms part of a car rally

streamlined smooth and gently curving. A streamlined object moves through air easily and quickly without producing a lot of air resistance

streamliner a high-speed motorbike with a slim, smooth, gently curving body around the whole bike and its rider. Streamliners are used to set speed records

supercar a very expensive high-performance car

supersonic faster than the speed of sound

V8 a type of car engine with eight cylinders

video equipment fitted to some police cars and police motorbikes for recording the view ahead

welded joined by melting together. Two pieces of metal are welded by heating them until they melt, run together, and set hard again

FIND OUT MORE

Websites

The website of the Indy Racing League:
http://www.indycar.com

A website to find out about drag racing in the UK:
www.santapod.co.uk

Lots of news and information about NASCAR racing:
http://www.nascar.com

The Formula 1 motor racing website:
http://www.formula1.com

Home of Australia's World Solar Challenge race for solar cars:
http://www.wsc.org.au

INDEX